W9-ADP-229

This book belongs to

_____

_____

_____

Country Living

Moments in Time

Engagement Calendar

HEARST BOOKS
New York

Copyright © 1994 by THE HEARST CORPORATION

All rights reserved. No part of this book may be reproduced or utilized in
any form or by any means, electronic or mechanical, including photocopying,
recording, or by any information storage or retrieval systems, without permission
in writing from the Publisher. Inquiries should be addressed to:
Permissions Department
William Morrow and Company, Inc.
1350 Avenue of the Americas
New York, N.Y. 10019

It is the policy of William Morrow and Company, Inc.,
and its imprints and affiliates, recognizing the importance of preserving
what has been written, to print the books we publish on acid-free paper,
and we exert our best efforts to that end.

ISBN: 0-688-13410-6

Printed in Singapore
First Edition
1 2 3 4 5 6 7 8 9 10

For Country Living
Rachel Newman, Editor-in-Chief
Niña Williams, Executive Editor
Julio Vega, Art Director
Mary R. Roby, Managing Editor
John Mack Carter, Director, Magazine Development

Produced by Smallwood and Stewart, Inc., New York City

Edited by Rachel Carley
Designed by Jan Melchior

Notice: Every effort has been made to locate the copyright owners of
the material used in this book. Please let us know if an error has been made,
and we will make any necessary changes in subsequent printings.

It's almost too cold
to hold a pen this
morning. I've lost a toe
since breakfast,
my nose is on its last
nostril. I've four
sweaters on (including
yours), two pairs
of trousers & socks, a
leather coat & a
dressing gown. Who was
the French poet who
had alphabetically lettered
underpants, & wore
every one up to H on a
cold morning?

DYLAN THOMAS

The first fall of snow is not only an event but it is a magical event. You go to bed in one kind of world and wake up to find yourself in another quite different, and if this is not enchantment, then where is it to be found?

J.B. PRIESTLEY

Foreword

The passage of the seasons is one of nature's most heartwarming gifts to us. Here in our office in the middle of Manhattan, it seems ironic that the changing seasons still trigger memories of times gone by and a keen anticipation of what is yet to come. When the first tender green leaf unfurls in spring, we eagerly organize all our warm-weather activities. And months later when that leaf slowly starts to blush, we think about the coming holidays, filling our calendars faster than the leaves can fall. Whether that tree dwells in a city, rooted in the hidden earth beneath a sheet of con-crete, or on a spacious hillside or in a dense forest, it serves as a cue, and on that cue we make our plans for a huge family feast or a solitary walk through the countryside.

It is with this in mind that we have put together this engagement calendar, because the weeks flow best when they are well planned. We have chosen some favorite images taken by our photographers here at *Country Living* to inspire you to celebrate the passage of time. For with every departure, as we see with the seasons, there is an arrival.

RACHEL NEWMAN
EDITOR-IN-CHIEF
COUNTRY LIVING

But I unfortunately was born at
the wrong end of time, and I have
to live *backwards* from in front.

T. H. WHITE

January

1

4

New Year's Day

2

5

3

6

January

7

10

8

11

9

12

January

13

16

14

17

15

18

January

19

22

20

23

21

24

January

25	28
26	29
27	30
	31

1

4

2

5

Groundhog Day

3

6

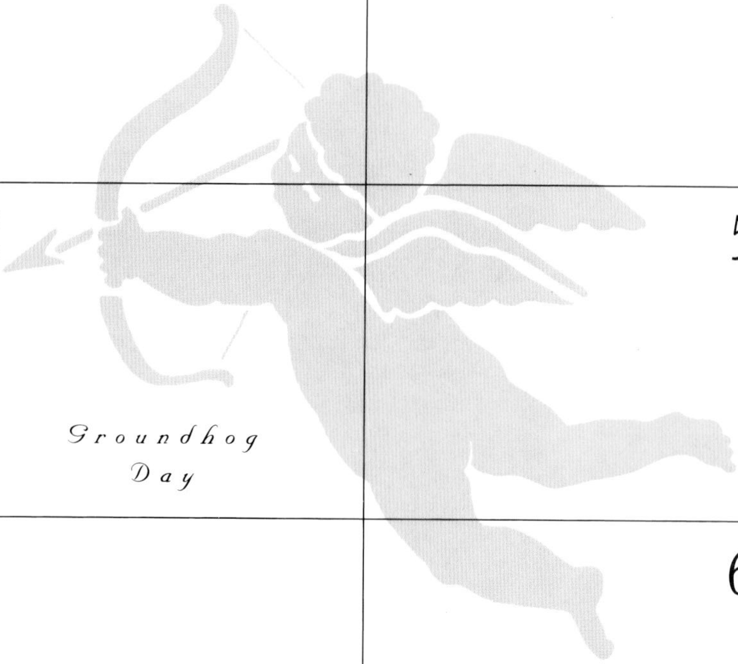

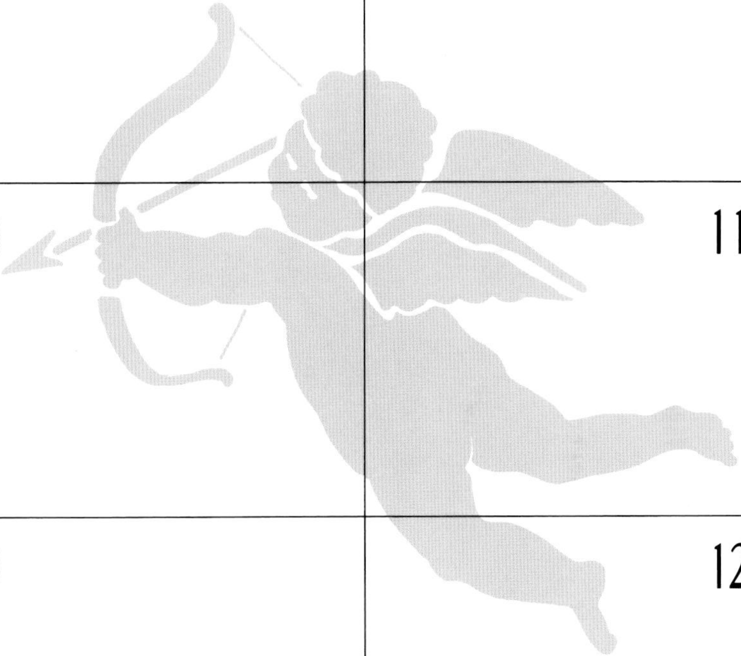

7

10

8

11

9

12

*Lincoln's
Birthday*

It is better to have
loafed and lost
than never to have
loafed at all.

JAMES THURBER

13

16

14

17

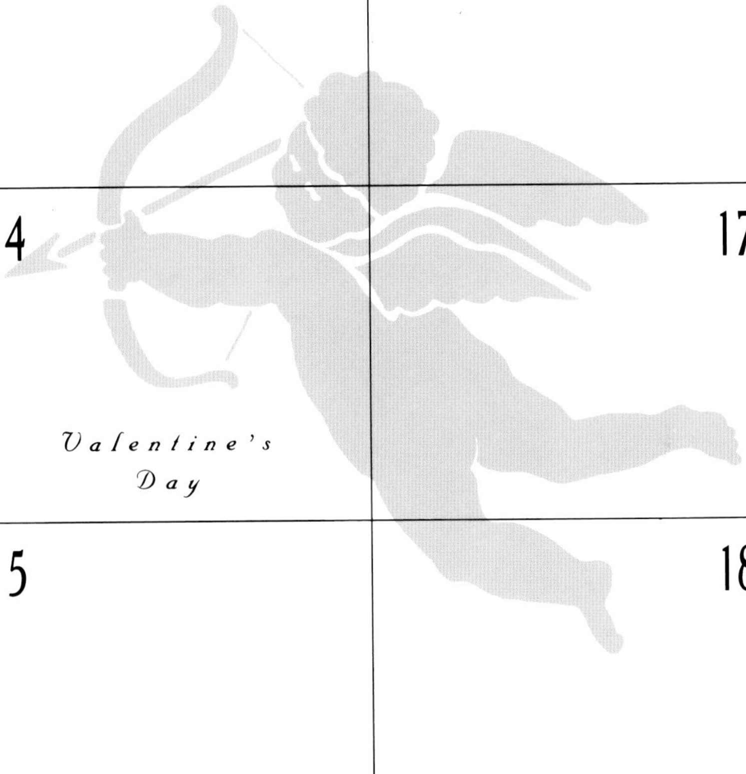

Valentine's Day

15

18

February

19	22
	Washington's Birthday
20	23
21	24

The cold was our pride, the snow was our beauty. It fell and fell, lacing day and night together in a milky haze, making everything quieter as it fell, so that winter seemed to partake of religion in a way no other season did, hushed, solemn.

PATRICIA HAMPL

February

25

28

26

27

I have at last got the little room I have wanted so long, and am very happy about it. It does me good to be alone.

LOUISA MAY ALCOTT

March

1

2

3

4

5

6

March

7

10

8

11

9

12

The planets, in congress
this month, hold sessions
most every day, and their
agreement is not very
complex. The state of the
weather will be very
fluctuating, jumping from
storm to sunshine and
from sunshine to storm,
rain, snow, and sleet.

NEW HAMPSHIRE ALMANAC,

MARCH 1888

March

13

16

14

17

St. Patrick's Day

15

18

March

19

22

20

23

21

24

Vernal
Equinox

March

25	28
26	29
27	30
	31

April

1	4
April Fool's Day	
2	5
3	6

7

10

8

11

9

12

13

16

14

17

15

18

The sun lay like a friendly arm across her shoulder.

MARJORIE KINNAN RAWLINGS

April

19	22
20	23
21	24

April

25

28

26

29

27

30

May

1	4
May Day	
2	5
3	6

7

10

8

11

9

12

May

13	16
14	17
15	18

May

19	22
	Armed Forces Day
20	23
21	24

May

25	28
26	29
27	30
	31

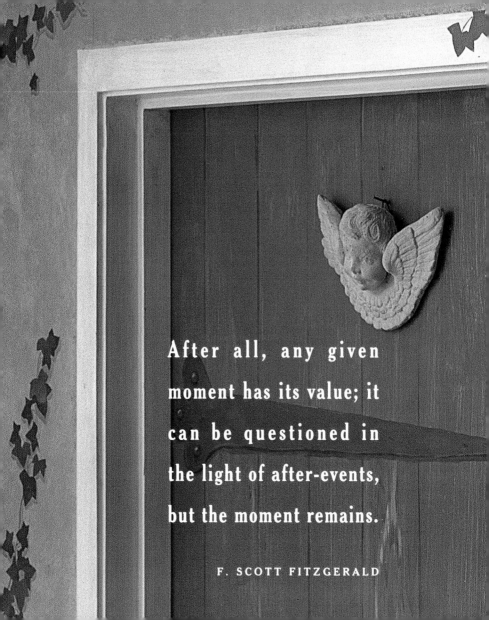

After all, any given moment has its value; it can be questioned in the light of after-events, but the moment remains.

F. SCOTT FITZGERALD

June

1

2

3

4

5

6

7

10

8

11

9

12

June

13

16

14

17

Flag Day

15

18

June

19	22
20	23
21	24

*Summer
Solstice*

I have loved the feel of green
grass under my feet . . . .

JOHN BURROUGHS

June

25	28
26	29
27	30

Alone, alone, all, all alone,

Alone on a wide, wide sea!

SAMUEL TAYLOR COLERIDGE

July

1	4
	Independence Day
2	5
3	6

Time is but the stream I go a-fishing in.

HENRY DAVID THOREAU

July

7	10
8	11
9	12

July

13	16
14	17
15	18

19

22

20

23

21

24

July

25	28
26	29
27	30
	31

1

4

2

5

3

6

7

10

8

11

9

12

August

13	16
14	17
15	18

August

19	22
20	23
21	24

This was one of those perfect
New England days in late
summer where the spirit of
autumn takes a first stealthy
flight, like a spy, through the
ripening country-side, and,
with feigned sympathy for
those who droop with August
heat, puts her cool cloak of
bracing air about leaf and
flower and human shoulders.

SARAH ORNE JEWETT

25

28

26

29

27

30

31

Then summer fades and passes . . .

THOMAS WOLFE

And pluck till time and
times are done
The silver apples
of the moon,
The golden apples
of the sun.

WILLIAM BUTLER YEATS

1

4

2

5

3

6

September

7	10
8	11
9	12

'Tis always
morning
somewhere.

HENRY
WADSWORTH
LONGFELLOW

13

16

14

17

15

18

19

22

Autumnal Equinox

20

23

21

24

25

28

26

29

27

30

I hate to be reminded
of the passage of
time, and in a garden
of flowers one can
never escape from it.
It is one of the charms
of a garden of grass
and evergreens, that
there for a while one is
allowed to hug the illu-
sion that time tarries.

E. V. LUCAS

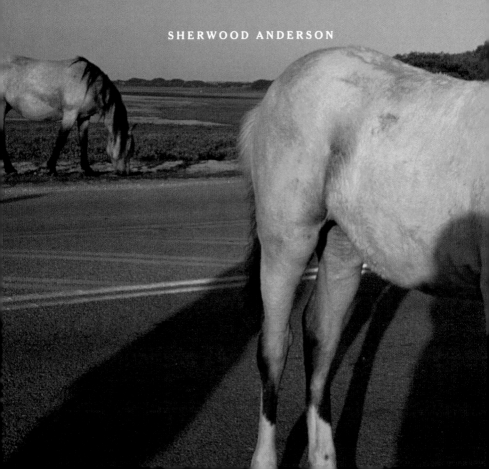

In the country sometimes I go about looking at horses and cattle. They eat grass, make love, work when they have to, bear their young. I am sick with envy of them.

SHERWOOD ANDERSON

One drifting yellow leaf on a windowsill
can be a city dweller's fall, pungent and melancholy
as any hillside in New England.

E. B. WHITE

1

4

2

5

3

6

October

7

10

8

11

9

12

Columbus
Day

13

16

14

17

15

18

19

22

20

23

21

24

October

25	28
26	29
27	30
	31
	Halloween

November

1

2

3

4

5

6

November

7	10
8	**11**
	Veterans Day
9	**12**

Time flies over us,
but leaves its shadow behind.

NATHANIEL HAWTHORNE

November

13

16

14

17

15

18

November

19	22
20	23
21	24

November

25	28
26	29
27	30

December

1

4

2

5

3

6

There's a certain slant of light
On winter afternoons...

EMILY DICKINSON

December

7

10

8

11

9

12

13

16

14

17

15

18

The pale,
cold light of the
winter sunset
did not
beautify—
it was like
the light
of truth itself.

WILLA CATHER

December

19	**22**
	Winter *Solstice*
20	**23**
21	**24**
	Christmas *Eve*

December

25	**28**
Christmas Day	
26	**29**
27	**30**
	31
	New Year's Eve

I find it difficult to believe in Father Christmas.
If he is the jolly old gentleman he is always said
to be, why doesn't he behave as such? How is it
that the presents so often go to the wrong people?

A. A. MILNE

Credits and Acknowledgments

Front cover ~ Photograph by Keith Scott Morton.

Title page ~ Photograph by Jessie Walker.

Frontispiece ~ Photograph by Keith Scott Morton. Excerpt from *The Sword in the Stone* by T. H. White.

Foreword ~ Photograph by Keith Scott Morton.

January ~ Photograph by Jessie Walker. Excerpt from *Apes and Angels* by J. B. Priestley. Photograph by Jessie Walker. Excerpt from *Letters to Vernon Watkins* by Dylan Thomas. Photograph by Keith Scott Morton.

February ~ Photograph by Keith Scott Morton. Excerpt from "The Courtship of Arthur and Al" by James Thurber. Excerpt from *A Romantic Education* by Patricia Hampl. Photograph by Keith Scott Morton. Photograph by Keith Scott Morton. Excerpt from *Mrs. Reinhardt* by Edna O'Brien.

March ~ Photograph by Keith Scott Morton. Excerpt from *Journals* by Louisa May Alcott. Excerpt from *New Hampshire Almanac*, March 1888, reprinted in *America and Her Almanacs* by Robb Sagendorph. Photograph by Gus Francisco and Allan Baillie. Photograph by Keith Scott Morton.

April ~ Photograph by Jessie Walker. Photograph by Doug Kennedy. Excerpt from *South Moon Under* by Marjorie Kinnan Rawlings. Photograph by Keith Scott Morton. Photograph by Elyse Lewin.

May ~ Photograph by Kari Haavisto. Photograph by Lilo Raymond. Photograph by Jessie Walker. Photograph by Jessie Walker. Excerpt from *The Crack Up* by F. Scott Fitzgerald.

June ~ Photograph by Paul Kopelow. Photograph by Jessie Walker. Excerpt by John Burroughs from *The Author's Kalandar, 1920* compiled by Anna C. Woodford. Photograph by Paul Kopelow. Photograph by Keith Scott Morton. Excerpt from "The Ancient Mariner" by Samuel Taylor Coleridge.

July ~ Photograph by Keith Scott Morton. Excerpt from *Walden* by Henry David Thoreau. Photograph by Paul Kopelow. Photograph by Keith Scott Morton. Photograph by Paul Kopelow.

August ~ Photograph by Keith Scott Morton. Photograph by Keith Scott Morton. Excerpt from "The Courting of Sister Wisby" by Sarah Orne Jewett, from *The Atlantic Monthly*, 1887. Photograph by Keith Scott Morton. Excerpt from *You Can't Go Home Again* by Thomas Wolfe.

September ~ Photograph by Keith Scott Morton. Excerpt from *The Song of Wandering Aengus* by William Butler Yeats. Photograph by Keith Scott Morton. Excerpt from "The Birds of Killingworth" by Henry Wadsworth Longfellow. Excerpt from *365 Days and One More* by E.V. Lucas. Photograph by Debra De Boise. Excerpt from *Letters of Sherwood Anderson* by Sherwood Anderson.

October ~ Photograph by Keith Scott Morton. Excerpt from *Every Day Is Saturday* by E. B. White. Photograph by Keith Scott Morton. Photograph by Joshua Greene. Photograph by Keith Scott Morton.

November ~ Photograph by Jessie Walker. Photograph by Keith Scott Morton. Excerpt from *The Marble Faun* by Nathaniel Hawthorne. Photograph by Al Teufen. Photograph by Keith Scott Morton.

December ~ Photograph by William Stites. Excerpt from *Selected Poems and Letters of Emily Dickinson* by Emily Dickinson. Excerpt from *My Antonia* by Willa Cather. Photograph by Keith Scott Morton. Excerpt from *Not That It Matters* by A. A. Milne. Photograph by Keith Scott Morton.